GETTING STARTED IN CRYPTOASSETS

By C. Y. Soh

Table of Contents

Introduction 1

CHAPTER1: Bitcoin 3

CHAPTER 2: The Blockchain 6

CHAPTER 3: Mining.. 8

CHAPTER 4: Alternative currencies/ Altcoins.....................15

CHAPTER 5: ICO & Whitepaper... 23

CHAPTER 6: Crypto currencies wallet 24

CHAPTER 7: Crypto currencies exchange...........................30

CHAPTER 8: Bitcoin Security... 33

CHAPTER 9: Trading...38

CHAPTER10: Regulatory and Tax Treatment..................... 52

Useful Website 61

FAQ.. 62

Introduction

In 2009 Bitcoin was introduced to the market at a value of 0.10 per coin. In 2013 it was valued at almost USD 1000 yet in 2015 it collapsed to USD 250 per coin due to hacking activities states Mt. Gox, the world's largest bitcoin exchange file for bankruptcy. Still, we notice that the price of bitcoin continues to rise and surpassed the price of an ounce of Gold in March 2017. In December 2017 its value peaked at USD 12,000 per coin making it one of the investments with the biggest return that I know off. The bitcoin grew tremendously in the 8 years since it first appeared on the market. Going from USD 0.10 to USD 12,000, that is a massive 120000% return on investment!

What is Cryptography?

Cryptography is the art of making text and messages unreadable to anyone other than the intended recipient by using coding techniques. It was first used by Mathematician Alan Turing during the Second World War. Turing's job was to decrypt the vastly complex German naval communications using his Enigma machine.

What is Crypto currency?

Simply put; crypto currency is a virtual currency that is used online for digital transactions. The word Crypto currency is derived from the word "Cryptography", referring to the consensus-keeping process guarded by strong cryptography. Crypto currencies are payment vehicles just like a normal everyday USD bank note. The difference is that the crypto currency solely serves the purpose of exchanging digital information through a process known as cryptography. Bitcoin is registered as the first ever-successful crypto currency and was invented by Satoshi Nakamoto. The success of the bitcoin birthed a slew of other types of crypto currencies competing against Bitcoin.

CHAPTER1: Bitcoin

Introduction to Bitcoin

In 2008 Satoshi Nakamoto published the bitcoin whitepaper called, Bitcoin: A peer-to-peer electronic Cash System. Till this day nobody knows who Satoshi Nakamoto is; since this name is only a pseudonym for either one person or a group of people. However, many are certain that this entity was the creator of Bitcoin and the bitcoin whitepaper which is available online at

https://bitcoin.org/bitcoin.pdf

How Do Bitcoin and other Cryptocurrencies Work?

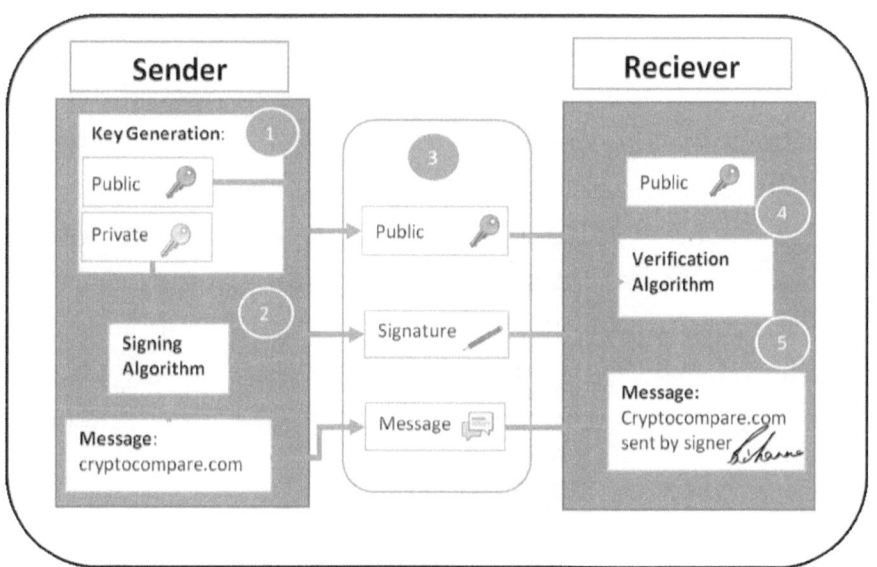

Source: cryptocompare.com

As is illustrated in the image above; the sender receives both a private and public key. The sender then signs the message with the signature and sends his/her public key, the signature and the message to the network (since the network is peer to peer every transaction in the network is validated by a full node). In the following step, the receiver or node checks that the message has been signed by the sender, using the verification algorithm. This action can only be done by the holder of the private key to the person receiving the public key.

Crypto currencies are very popular right now because the developer of the bitcoin Satoshi Nakamoto successfully found a way to build decentralized digital cash system that opened the door for other crypto currencies to be developed.

What is a decentralized cash system?

A decentralized system is a system that is powered by its users without having any third party, central or financial authority controlling it, which means that no central bank or government has power over this system. The problem with a centralized network in a payment system is the so called "double spending". Double spending occurs when customers spends the same amount twice. For instance, when purchasing stuff online, often time you have to incur for unnecessary and expensive transaction fees. Usually, this is done by a central server that keeps track of your balances.

This is most commonly known as the Blockchain Technology.

Bitcoin supply

Bitcoins are created each time a user discovers a new block. New blocks creation happens after a total of 2016 blocks have been mined to aim for a constant two week adjustment period (equivalent to 6 per hour.) The amount of bitcoins generated per block is set to decrease geometrically, resulting in a 50% reduction after every 210,000 blocks, or after approximately four years of block creation. This results in the fact that the amount of bitcoins in existence never exceeds 21 million. Speculated justifications for the unintuitive value "21 million" are that it matches a 4-year reward halving schedule; or the ultimate total number of Satoshi's that will be mined is close to the maximum capacity of a 64-bit floating point number. Satoshi has never really justified or explained many of these constants.

$$\frac{\sum_{i=0}^{32} 210000 \lfloor \frac{50.10^8}{2^i} \rfloor}{10^8}$$

Bitcoin halving

As soon as a newly discovered block is added to the bitcoin network, a fresh amount of bitcoins are gifted to the miner who discovered the valid block. Initially miners received 50 BTC, but that amount was reduced to 25 BTC in late 2012 and dropped again to 12.5 BTC in 2016, after another 210000 block. This event is known as "halving". One can view the live bitcoin halving clock online at http://www.bitcoinblockhalf.com/

This dictates that after every 210,000 blocks, the amount of new coin released should suddenly be cut in half. As the code runs, it continues to calculate how many blocks have been solved. When the number hits 210,000, the first halving event takes place.

CHAPTER 2: The Blockchain

Blockchain technology is all about managing and maintaining a growing set of data blocks. This can be done by using the decentralized aka P2P (Peer to Peer) network. In blockchain technology, edits or changes cannot be made to a recorded piece of data.

To put it in simpler terms, it enables you to send a gold coin via email. The P2P network is a consensus network. It is a system that offers a new payment method for the transactions of digital currencies. Let's check out an example. A crypto currency like Bitcoin has its own network of peers. Every peer has a record of the complete history of all transactions as well as the balance of every account. Upon confirmation of every transaction, almost everyone in the whole network will be notified of the transaction. Every transaction goes through the same process where A gives X amount of Bitcoins to B, and then signed off by A's private key. After signed, a transaction is broadcasted in the network. The information is sent from one peer to every other peer on the network.

One of the most important stages in the cryptocurrency system is confirmation. All transactions depends on confirmation. When the transaction is not confirmed, it is vulnerable to hacking and forging practices. When a transaction is confirmed, it is stored permanently. It cannot be reversed, it is impossible to be hacked, it is not forgeable as it is part of a permanent record of the historical transaction: The Blockchain. The blockchain can be viewed as an online ledger, where all transactions are recorded and made visible to the entire network. This proves that crypto currencies are secured by complex mathematical equations rather than people or trust. This process is very secure and it's highly unlikely that the address of a currency is forged. The role of miners is to confirm transactions in the crypto currency network thus they are the only one who can do that. Miners record transactions, verify them and disperse the transactional information in the network. For every completed transaction monitored and facilitated by the miners, they are rewarded with a token of crypto currency as is done with bitcoin. Since miners must deliver such impeccable results in the crypto currency system all the time, let's look at their role in more detail.

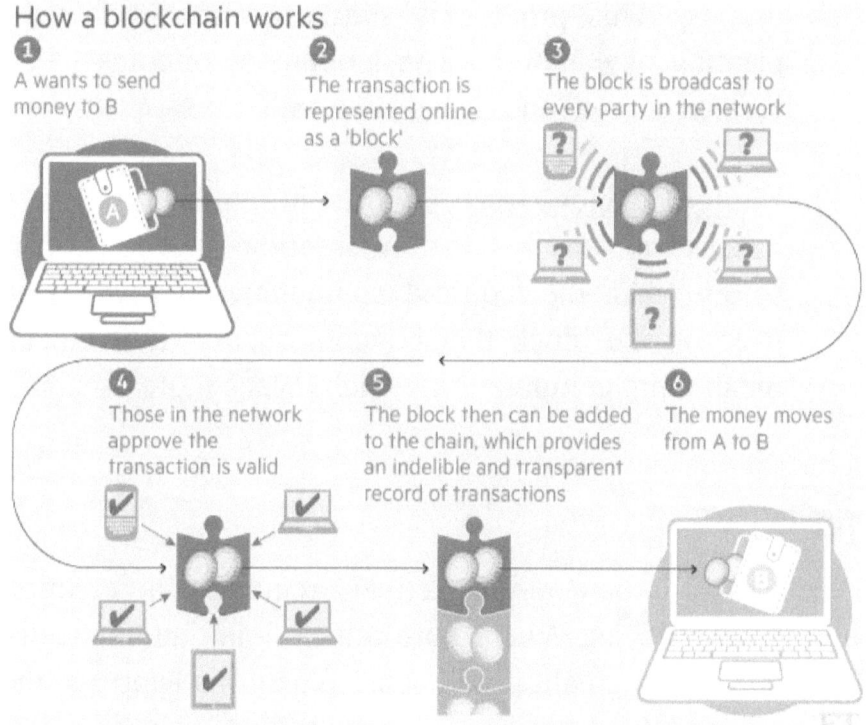

How a blockchain works

① A wants to send money to B

② The transaction is represented online as a 'block'

③ The block is broadcast to every party in the network

④ Those in the network approve the transaction is valid

⑤ The block then can be added to the chain, which provides an indelible and transparent record of transactions

⑥ The money moves from A to B

Source: www.weforum.org

CHAPTER 3: Mining

The Bitcoin system is entirely based on computation. Transactions are packed into blocks, a process that gobbles up fast amounts of computation to "prove" (or "confirm"), but only a small amount of computation to verify as "proven", in a process called mining.

Mining serves two purposes in Bitcoin blockchain network:

1. <u>Fresh bitcoins are created in each blocks due to mining</u>: This process is similar to a central bank printing new money. The amount of bitcoins to be created is fixed and diminishes with time.

2. <u>Mining develops trust:</u> the trust in mining skyrockets because it ensures that transactions are confirmed solely when the required computational power was used on the block that contains them. More blocks mean more computation, which means more trust.

Mining Difficulty

Bitcoin nodes when mining actively regulates the creation pace of new blocks. When more miners join, automatically the rate of block creation will soar. When this happens, the mining difficulty that rises is compensated, resulting in a decrease of the rate of block creation.

new blocks must be created in no more than 10 minutes (Ten minutes was specifically chosen by Satoshi Nakamoto as a tradeoff between fast confirmation time and the amount of work wasted due to chain splits and orphan blocks. The regulation is done by periodically adjusting the hash target value for blocks.

After every 2,016 blocks (which ideally spans every 2 weeks, with each block taking 10 minutes to confirm) Bitcoin nodes produces a new difficulty accordingly, based on the time it took to mine the last 2,016 blocks.

Rewards for mining services

Solving the Proof of Work problem requires a lot of computing power and that power costs money. To encourage participants to invest their resources in mining, Bitcoin built a rewarding system for successfully mined block (plus the transaction fees of the transactions contained in the new block).

When a block is discovered, the person who discovered it, will be awarded a certain number of bitcoins, upon agreement with the rest of the network. Currently this bounty is 12.5 bitcoins. Based on Bitcoin's algorithm, this bounty divides itself every 210,000 blocks (i.e. approximately every 4 years). This means that by the year 2140, the reward will be removed entirely when the limit of 21 million bitcoins is reached asymptotically. Transactional processing will from then on only be rewarded by transactional fees. Additionally, the miner is awarded the fees paid by Bitcoin users sending transactions.

Pool mining

Mining pools collect all of the hashing from miners and basically run them off of one account. When a block is found, the mining pool's wallet is the one that gets the payment, and then the payments are split and distributed into each miner's site account based on their personal contribution towards finding the block. For example, if a miner contributed half of the pool's shares into finding the new block, they would get half of the block reward.

Mining Hardware

CPU mining: This is the process first used by Satoshi. Back then Bitcoin client software did mining on a user's PC (i.e. CPU mining), however with technological improvements everything has changed to more efficient mining hardware.

GPU mining: GPUs (i.e. Graphics Processing Units on Graphics cards) are used for lots of mathematical calculations in parallel and are orders of magnitude faster than CPUs

FPGA (Field Programmable Gate Arrays): An intermediate step between a fast processor and a dedicated ASIC, FPGAs were used until ASICs emerged and dominated Bitcoin mining

ASIC mining: ASICs (Application-Specific Integrated Circuits) are custom built for a particular application and are thus orders of magnitude faster than GPUs, which are general-purpose. In Bitcoin, these chips are customized to only perform SHA-256 hashing.

Proof of Work (PoW) and Proof of Stake (PoS)

What is proof of work?

Proof of work is a specific algorithm that is used to confirm transactions and produce new blocks to the chain. The PoW system allows miners to compete against each other to complete transactions on the network and get rewarded. In network users send each other digital tokens. A decentralized ledger gathers all the transactions into blocks. However, care should be taken to confirm the transactions and arrange blocks. This responsibility bears on special node called miners, and the process is called mining. The main working principles are a complicated mathematical puzzle and a possibility to easily prove the solution.

What is a proof of stake?

Proof of stake also validates transactions to achieve the distribution consensus. Just like the proof of work, it is merely an algorithm with the exact same purpose but with a slightly different process. The first time the idea of Proof of stake was brought to people's attention was on the bitcoin talk forum in 2011, but in 2012 peercoin became the first digital currency to use this method, together with ShadowCash, Nxt, BlackCoin, NuShares/NuBits, Qora and Nav Coin.

With the proof of stake method, creators of new blocks are chosen in a deterministic manner, taking wealth into consideration. This differs from the proof of work where the algorithm rewards miners who encrypt messages with the goal of validating transactions and creating new blocks. Also, all the digital currencies are previously created in the beginning, and their number never changes.

This means that in the PoS system there is no block reward, so, the miners take the transaction fees. This is why, in fact, in this PoS system miners are called forgers instead. In a distributed consensus-based on the proof of Work, miners need a lot of energy. One Bitcoin transaction required the same amount of electricity as powering 1.57 American households for one day (data from 2015). And these energy costs are paid with fiat currencies, leading to a constant downward pressure on the digital currency value.

Experts believe that by 2020 bitcoin transactions may consume as much electricity as Denmark.

This is a problem for many developers, thus leading the Ethereum community to lean towards the proof of stake method for a greener and cheaper distributed form of consensus.

Moreover, rewards for the creation of a new block are different: with Proof-of-Work. It is possible that the miner never owns any of the digital currency he/she is mining. In Proof-of-Stake, forgers are always those who own the coins minted.

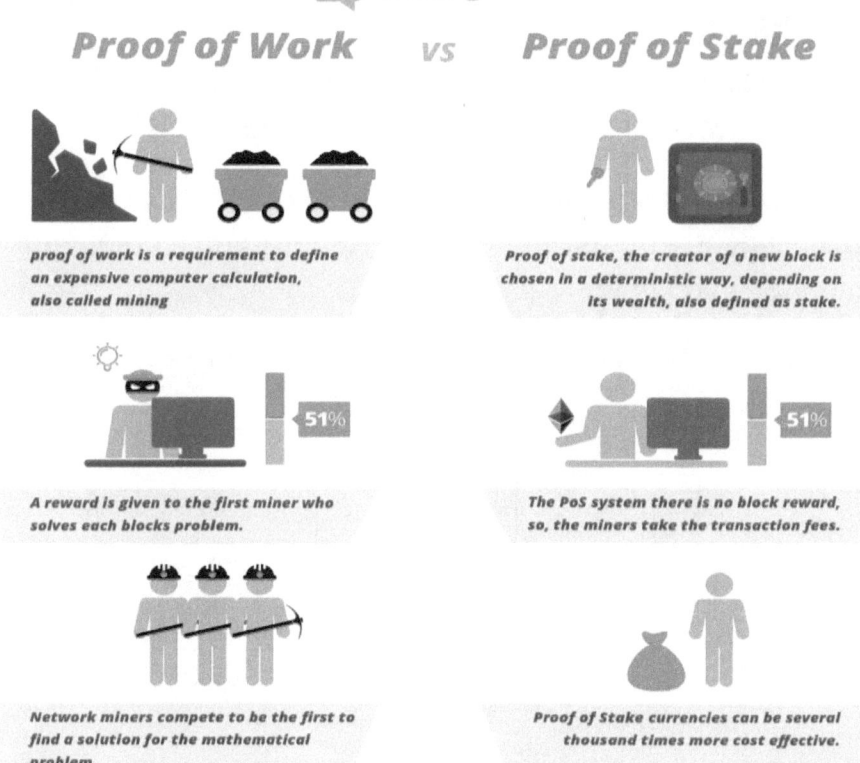

Proof of Work vs Proof of Stake

proof of work is a requirement to define an expensive computer calculation, also called mining

Proof of stake, the creator of a new block is chosen in a deterministic way, depending on its wealth, also defined as stake.

A reward is given to the first miner who solves each blocks problem.

The PoS system there is no block reward, so, the miners take the transaction fees.

Network miners compete to be the first to find a solution for the mathematical problem

Proof of Stake currencies can be several thousand times more cost effective.

Source: https://blockgeeks.com/guides/proof-of-work-vs-proof-of-stake/

Hard fork

The split of one single crypto currency into two is called a hard fork. This is due to changes in a crypto currency's existing code, resulting in an old and new version. A soft fork is basically the same thing, but here only one blockchain (and thus one coin) will remain valid as users adopt the update. So both fork types create a split, but a hard fork delivers two blockchain/coins and a soft fork delivers only one. Segwit was a soft fork, Bitcoin Cash, Bitcoin Gold, and Segwit2x are all hard forks.

The result is generally (to use the words of Coinbase when discussing a User Activated Soft Fork):

One blockchain will dominate, pushing the other block chain to have low community adoption and value.

Both block chains are adopted, co-existing and operating independently of one another with roughly equal community adoption and value.

In general, the 1st one tends is the expected outcome of a hard fork.

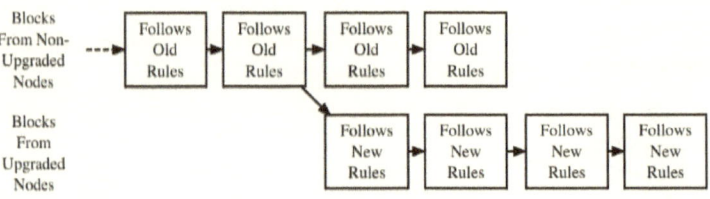

Source: Investopedia

Soft forks

Soft forks are change to the Bitcoin protocol wherein updated nodes start operating with new rules, while older nodes never change. Old nodes still keep receiving new blocks and will recognize them as valid, so we can say that a soft fork is backwards-compatible. Soft forked nodes don't have major impact on the updated parts of the network, but they're still part of it.

CHAPTER 4: Alternative currencies/ Altcoins

The word "Altcoin" is a combination of two words: "alt" and "coin"; alt stands for alternative and coin signifies currency. Altcoins are therefore a category of crypto currency that is alternative to the Bitcoin. After Bitcoin's success, many other peer-to-peer digital currencies were created in the hope to imitate bitcoin's success.

Most of these altcoins are built up on Bitcoin's framework; therefore most altcoins are peer-to-peer, involving a mining process and offering efficient and cheap ways to carry out transactions on the web. Yet many altcoins still vary widely from each other.

A great source for information on all the available Altcoins is https://coinmarketcap.com/ . Another good website which analyze Altcoins in detail is https://coincheckup.com/coins/cardano/purpose

Bitcoin has always been the favorite in the universe of crypto currency. Till recently, fiat currencies where majorly used until virtual currencies proved to serve as a very important purpose in the investment realm and people started opting for crypto currencies instead of fiat currencies.

Believe it or not, aside from Bitcoin, over 1000 crypto currencies are in rotation! However, we will only discuss some of the most prominent currencies in the market.

Ethereum

Ethereum became the second biggest crypto currency in just a couple of years. It was created by Vitalik Buterin and was launched in 2015. It is the only crypto currency believed to surpass Bitcoin in the future.

Is Ethereum similar to Bitcoin?

In a way it is, but not entirely. Like Bitcoin, Ethereum is a part of a blockchain network. The difference is on the focus. Bitcoin's blockchain focuses on tracking ownership of the digital currency while Ethereum blockchain focuses on running the programming code or network. This shift in focus enables Ethereum to develop thousands of different applications in a single platform, instead of having to build an entirely original blockchain for each new application. In the Ethereum blockchain, miners earn Ethers. Ether is ethereum's crypto token that helps run the network.

Ethereum's greatest benefit is that its blockchain is able to decentralize any services that are centralized e.g. loans provided by banks, online transactions using PayPal, voting systems and so much more.

With Ethereum one can also build a Decentralized Autonomous Organization (DAO). A DAO is a fully autonomous organization without a leader. DAOs are run by programming codes on a collection of smart contracts written in the Ethereum blockchain. DAOs were built to replace the traditional organizational structure and like Bitcoin; eliminate the need for people and a centralized control.

What are the most obvious benefits of Ethereum?

1. No third party can make any changes to the data. The system was built to be tamper and corruption proof (This is because Ethereum is built based on a network formed around a consensus as a result, making censorship impossible).
2. Just like Bitcoin, Ethereum is backed up by secure cryptography. Therefore, the applications are well protected against any form of hacking.

Ripple

Ripple is more than a crypto currency. It is a technology equipped with a dual function which are digital currency and digital payment network for financial transactions. The company was launched in 2012 and co-founded by Chris Larsen and Jed McCaleb. The Ripple token is called the XRP.

Ripple differs from all other crypto currencies as it operates on an open-source and a peer-to-peer decentralized platform which allows money to be transferred in both fiat and crypto currency form. However, a middleman is needed during transactions. This middleman or medium serves as a gateway or link, connecting parties wanting to make a transaction. The way it works is that the Gateway functions as a credit intermediary that receives and sends currencies to public addresses over the Ripple network. Ripple's digital coin, XRP acts as a bridge for other currencies which includes both fiat and crypto currencies.

Ripple's network is built to exchange any currency between one another. If one user chooses Bitcoins as the form of payment for his services from a second user, then second user does not necessarily have to possess Bitcoins. The second user can pay the amount owed to the first user through his/her Gateway with US Dollars or any other currencies. The first user will then receive Bitcoins converted from the US Dollars from his Gateway.

Even though one is able to exchange it into any other currencies, the Ripple network does not run with a proof-of-work system like Bitcoin. Instead, transactions are heavily reliant on a consensus protocol in order to validate account balances and transactions on the system. But Ripple does improve some features of traditional banks. Namely, transactions are completed within seconds on a Ripple network even though the system handles millions of transactions frequently. Unlike traditional banks, even a wire transfer may take up days or weeks to complete. The fee to conduct transactions on Ripple is also very minimal, as opposed to large fees charged by banks to complete cross-border payments.

Litecoin

Litecoin was launched in 2011 with high aspirations to be the "silver to bitcoin's "gold". Litecoin is also the second crypto currency after bitcoin to record the highest market cap of any mined crypto currency at one point of time. The main reason of Litecoin's creation is to make up what Bitcoin lacked.

Litecoin and Bitcoin are more or less the same. There sole difference is the 2.5 minute time to generate a block for Litecoin, as opposed to Bitcoin's 10 minutes. However, miners and technical experts argues that the speed is but a small difference, but most important difference is that Litecoin possesses a more improved work algorithm which speeds up the hashing power and system altogether.

Due to its algorithm, Litecoin can handle a higher volume of transactions. The faster block time also prevents double spending attacks. Even though Litecoin couldn't become the second best crypto currency, it is still actively mined and traded and is bought by investors as a backup in case Bitcoin fails.

Dash

Dash was first launched as XCoin (XCO) on January 18, 2014. A couple of weeks later on February 28, the name was changed to "Darkcoin." On March 25, 2015, Darkcoin was rebranded as "Dash.", which stands for "Digital Cash".

Within the first two days of launch, 1.9 million coins were mined, which is approximately 10% of the total supply that will ever be issued. Creator and lead developer of Dash, Evan Duffield, attributed this to a bug created when the Litecoin code was forked to create Dash, "which incorrectly converted the difficulty, then tried using a corrupt value to calculate the subsidy once the problem was resolved. Evan wanted to re-launch the coin, but the community overwhelmingly disapproved. He suggested an "airdrop" of coins in order to broaden the initial distribution but the community also disapproved of this proposal. As such, the initial distribution was left alone and development of the project continued.

The majority of mined coins were distributed on crypto currency exchanges in the following months at very low price levels. The Dash Core Team, responsible for developing the currency, has since grown and its network is maintained by many master nodes worldwide. All Core Team employees are paid from Dash's budget system and therefore are not reliant on donations or sponsorships that can lead to conflicts of interest.

Masternodes

Dash functions on a two- tier network. On the first tier network new blocks are created which is handled by miners. The second tier of the Dash network consists of "masternodes" which perform PrivateSend, InstantSend, and governance functions.

Masternodes require 1000 DASH as collateral to prevent Sybil attacks. That collateral can be spent at any time, but doing so removes the associated masternode from the network. Because masternodes provide vital network functions, the block reward is split between miners and masternodes, with each group earning 45% of the block reward. The remaining 10% of each block reward funds the "budget" or "treasury" system.

Monero

This crypto currency was launched in 2014 to create an algorithm that added the privacy features that was missing in Bitcoin. Monero invented a system known as the "ring signatures" to conceal the identity of its senders and recipients. Ring signatures combine a user's private account keys with public keys obtained from Monero's blockchain to create a ring of possible signers that would not allow outsiders to link a signature to a specific user.

Monero is all about privacy. It gives users the ability to keep their transactions private, but can also share their information selectively if needed. All Monero accounts are utilized with a "view key", which allows anyone holding it to view the account's transactions. Initially, the ring signature system concealed the senders and recipients involved in the Monero transactions without hiding the amount being transferred.

However, an updated and improved version of the ring signature system known as "Ring CT" enabled the value of individual transactions as well as its recipients to be hidden. Apart from ring signatures, Monero also improved its privacy settings by using "Stealth Addresses", which are randomly generated, one time addresses. These addresses are created for each transaction on behalf of the recipients. With this feature, the recipients use a single address and transactions they receive go to separate, unique addresses. This way, Monero transactions cannot be linked to the published address of the recipients. By providing a high level of privacy Monero allows each unit of its individual currency to be exchanged between one another. Meaning, each of its coin has the same value. Like the other crypto currencies, Monero offers interested parties to mine block. Individuals may choose to join a mining pool, or they may mine Monero by themselves.

Anyone with a computer can mine Monero, for it doesn't require any specific hardware or specific integrated circuits like Bitcoin. Monero uses a Proof-of-Work (PoW) Algorithm that can accept a wide range of processors. This feature was carefully thought out and included to ensure that mining was open to all parties. Monero is especially popular within multiple dark web marketplaces and has generated its own fan base due to its privacy settings.

CHAPTER 5: ICO & Whitepaper

ICO stands for Initial Coin Offering

The term ICO refers to the actions a crypto currency startup take when it wants to raise funding to further the development of their coin. The startup distributes a set amount of their coins (often referred to as "tokens") to investors, who purchase these tokens hoping that the project succeeds and those coins gain value. If for some reasons the coins do not gain value, the money invested is returned to the investors.
ICOs, unlike IPOs, are unregulated and so great care should be taken before participating in one to make sure that it is not a scam.

The future of altcoins

Altcoins are still very new and therefore still as unpredictable as they are exciting. All top altcoins are in the race to take the top spot from bitcoin, while attempting to carve their own niches. Their goal remains which is to reimagine the way we do business, how we send and receive money, and how we transfer assets like properties and cars.

CHAPTER 6: Crypto currencies wallet

"A wallet is software that holds all your addresses. Use it to send bitcoins and manage your keys." (from Antonopoulos, Mastering Bitcoin)

Simply put, a wallet is like your own crypto-currency bank. It enables you to send, receive and securely store different kinds of crypto currencies. Your wallet also stores the public and private keys for your crypto-currency. Your public keys are the address you use to send or receive crypto currency. The beauty of this is that public keys can't be hacked, so you can show them to people. The private keys are what actually allow you to access your crypto! Without your private keys, you can't use your crypto-currency, it is essentially worthless. Even the private keys are not to be worried about because they are all automatically taken care of behind the scenes by your crypto currency wallet. There are two main categories of wallets: *A hot wallet and a cold storage wallet.*

A hot wallet is basically any kind of online wallet. To access this type of wallet, you need to be connected to the internet. Because of this, a hot wallet is not as secure and is more vulnerable to hacking and malware. This kind of wallet is best used for trading funds or a small amount of crypto-currency for everyday transactions. Think of it as your short term crypto-currency checking account.

A cold storage wallet is a crypto-currency wallet that is stored offline. It doesn't need to be connected to the internet and is mostly used on a limited basis. This wallet is much safer than the hot wallet and thus appropriate for the storage of large amounts of crypto-currency. Think of this wallet as your long term crypto-currency savings account or even similar to a safe for your precious metals.

TWO KINDS OF HOT WALLETS

Online/Exchange wallet

To get an online (hot) wallet, you have to sign up through someone's website. One way to automatically get one is to create a coin base account. The only benefit these wallets have is that they are very easy to use. Web wallets are the most unsecure wallets and susceptible to hacking putting your email and login info at a high risk for theft. Furthermore, the wallet operator also controls the private keys for your crypto-currency. While this may seem plausible, it actually puts you at high risk, because if they ever lose your keys or they get hacked or stolen, you can kiss your crypto goodbye. Just do a quick Google search for "Mt Gox bitcoin exchange" and you'll see some horror stories of people who got their bitcoin stolen in a similar situation. Therefore, it is advised to only use this kind of wallet as an entry point or for the storage of a small amount of crypto-currency for everyday transactions on Amazon or something similar.

Software wallet:

The software wallet can be downloaded to your computer or mobile phone. While it may not provide complete protection, its safer than a hot wallet because you are in total control of your crypto-currency and private keys and not some other party. However, this kind of wallet is as safe as your computer, meaning your crypto can still be stolen if your computer is hacked or gets infected with certain types of malware. It is best to only use this type of wallet for short term storage, holding crypto funds you plan on trading, or for storage of a small amount of crypto-currency for everyday transactions. If you still decide to store a large amount of crypto-currency in your software wallet, I would advise to buy a computer specifically for transactions related to your wallet. Never use it for other activities like checking emails, watching videos or doing anything else online. Your chances of getting hacked or infected with malware will be greatly diminished.

TWO KINDS OF COLD STORAGE WALLETS

Hardware wallet

A hardware wallet is an offline wallet that is usually some sort of USB device. You can connect it to the internet when necessary but can be disconnected from the internet and made totally unavailable to hackers or malware. You can store this type of wallet anywhere you like. This kind of wallet is super secure, way more than a hot wallet. Even when connected to a computer, this type of wallet stays secure making it impossible to get hacked or infected with malware because the private key has already been generated while offline. Two of the famous hardware wallets are Trezor and Nano Ledger.

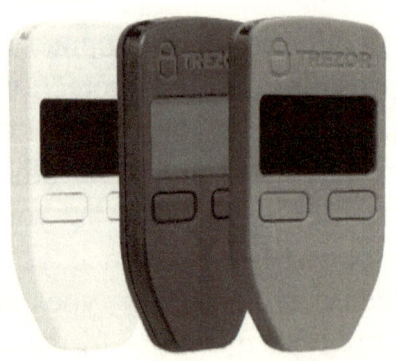 

Paper wallet

With a paper wallet, you basically print out your public and private keys. Yep, print them out on real paper. Store it safely so you don't have to lose that piece of paper. Make sure it is never in the vicinity of water and fire. Store it in a safe. Make multiple copies. Hackers can't touch your paper wallet but thieves and forgetfulness can. One way to turn your Bitcoin into a paper wallet is by using BitcoinPaperWallet.com

this was basic info on wallets to help you get started. We recommend you keep your crypto-currency off the exchanges and have a small amount in software wallets (your crypto bank checking account) and a larger amount in your hardware's wallet (your crypto bank savings account).

Today there are lots of different wallet solutions, allowing users to choose what best suits them, for example:

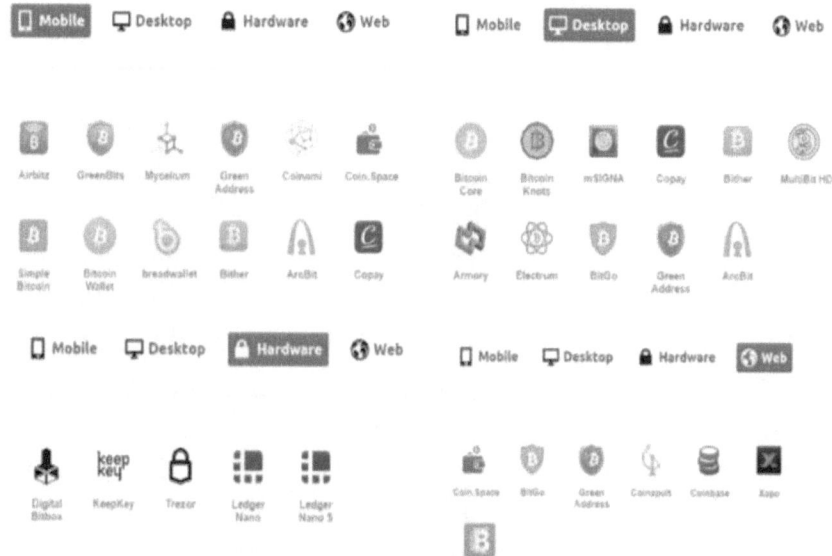

Source: https://bitcoin.org/en/choose-your-wallet

Sending and Receiving bitcoins

The following are some of the ways you can receive your bitcoins:

1. Offer a Service or Product for bitcoins. There are many ways you can go about this and many businesses and individuals already accept bitcoins.
2. Accept bitcoins as a donation. You can accept bitcoins for your charity.
3. Purchase bitcoins through an Exchange e.g. to get relatively large amounts of bitcoins at the current market price.
4. A very comprehensive list of Bitcoin exchanges, categorized by country, can be found here. Identity verification will typically be required before you can buy/sell bitcoins and deposit/withdraw fiat currencies. Thus, it might take some time.

One other significant way to get bitcoins is faucets. A list of faucets can be found here: https://99bitcoins.com/top-10-bitcoin-faucets/.You may get a few bits (1/1,000,000 of a BTC) for free, however, most faucets are not operational anymore. Stay away from faucet asking for some kind of activity in exchange of Bitcoins.

When first created, a Bitcoin wallet is empty thus receiving bitcoins can only happen when you have provided the sender with your wallets Bitcoin address. The process is just like sending an email; in order to receive an email we have to give our email address to someone who wants to send us an email. To send bitcoins to e.g. a client when using a desktop, a sender can just copy and paste the receiver's address, for eg:

16NxtXigsqxWM8T9Pho8dbwNc1cufrcL23

If the sender is using a mobile client, it could be more convenient to scan the relevant QR code:

CHAPTER 7: Crypto currencies exchange

It is important to know that a bitcoin exchange is different from a bitcoin wallet. A bitcoin exchange offers a platform where bitcoin buyers and sellers can transact with each other. A bitcoin wallet serves only as a digital storage service where bitcoin holders can securely store their coins. To be more technical, bitcoin wallets store private keys which are used to authorize transactions and access the bitcoin address of a user. Most bitcoin exchanges provide bitcoin wallets for their users, but may charge a fee for this service. Many buyers can easily find sellers on exchange platforms. These exchange platforms function similarly to traditional stock exchange market where traders can opt to buy and sell bitcoin by inputting either a market order or a limit order. If a market order is selected, the trader opts to exchange his coins for the most attractive price in the marketplace. With a limit order set, the trader directs the exchange to trade coins for a price below the current ask or above the current bid, depending on whether s/he is buying or selling.

For example, on a bitcoin exchange, three sellers are asking for BTC/USD 9265.75, BTC/USD 9269.55, and BTC/USD 9270.00. A trader who is interested can start a market order to purchase bitcoins at the best price of $9265.75. If the trader can only own five bitcoins for the best ask and 10 coins are available for $9269.55, and the trader wants to buy 10 at market value, his order will be filled with 5 coins @ $9265.75 and the remaining 5 @ $9269.55.

If a trader thinks that he can get a more lucrative deal on the bitcoins, he could set a limit order for, say, $9660.10. If a seller choose to match or set a lower ask price with this order, then the buyer will get filled. Online bitcoin marketplaces usually designate bitcoin participants as either makers or takers. If a buyer or seller place a limited order, automatically it is added to his/her order book until the price is matched by another trader on the opposite end of the transaction. The buyer, who matches the price, is called the maker. A price taker is a trader who places a market order that immediately gets filled.

All bitcoin exchange, transaction fees must be paid for every successfully completed buy and sell order carried out within the exchange. This fee depends on the amount of bitcoin transactions that is conducted. For example, bitcoin exchange Poloniex has its rate ranging from 0 to 0.25%, GDAX fees range from 0 to 0.30%, Kraken's fees range from 0 to 0.36%, and Paxful charges 1% of the amount of a sale to the seller but buyers don't get charged.

To transact in bitcoin on an exchange, a user has to register with the exchange and go through a lengthy verification processes to authenticate his or her identity. Once the authentication is successful, an account is opened for the user who then has to transfer funds into this account before coins purchased can be made. Every exchange has its own payment method that can be used for depositing funds including bank wires, direct bank transfers, credit or debit cards, bank drafts, money orders, and even gift cards. If a trader wishes to withdraw money from his account he could do that by using the options provided by his exchange which could include a bank transfer, PayPal transfer, check mailing, cash delivery, bank wire, or credit card transfer.

For every withdrawal or deposit, there is a fee attached, which depends on the payment method chosen to transfer funds. If the risk associated with this chargeback from a payment medium is high, the higher the fee will be. Making a bank draft or wiring money to the exchange has a lesser risk of a chargeback compared to funding your account with PayPal or a credit/debit card where the funds being transferred can be reversed and returned to the user upon his/her request to the bank.

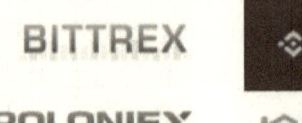  

CHAPTER 8: Bitcoin Security

It is very important so keep your wallet secured at all time. Bitcoin allows you to make transactions from anywhere very easily and allows you to be in control of your money. Such great features also come with great security concerns. However, if used correctly, Bitcoin will provide very high levels of security, but never forget that **you are responsible for the safety and security of your money.**

Be careful with online services

Stay clear from any online services promising to store your money online. Many exchanges and online wallets experienced security breaches in the past and till today such services do not provide enough insurance and security, thus lacking the ability to store money like a bank. Accordingly, you might want to use other types of Bitcoin wallets. Otherwise, you should choose such services very carefully. Additionally, using two-factor authentication is highly recommended.

Small amounts for everyday uses

A Bitcoin wallet is literally a wallet with digital money. It is therefore important to treat it as such and not store a high amount of bitcoins in it. It is in every sense of the word better to keep only small amounts of bitcoins on your computer, mobile, or other electronic device for immediate usage while keeping the rest of your bitcoins in a more secure environment or device.

Backup your wallet

A backup of your wallet will come in handy if you experience a sudden computer failure or other risks such as hacking or malware. It can also allow you to recover your wallet after your mobile or computer was stolen when you keep your wallet encrypted. Make sure to store it in a safe and secure place.

Backup your entire wallet

Some wallets use many hidden private keys internally. It is therefore wise to make a backup of your entire wallet. A backup of the private keys for your visible Bitcoin addresses, might result in crypto loss and you might not be able to recover a great part of your funds with your backup.

Encrypt online backups

Anything that is stored online is highly vulnerable to theft. Even a computer that is connected to the Internet is at high risk for malicious softwares. Thus encrypting any backup that is exposed to the network is a good security practice.

Use many secure locations

Single points of failure are bad for security. If your backup is not dependent on a single location, it is less likely that any bad event will prevent you to recover your wallet. You might also want to consider using different Medias like USB keys, papers and CDs.

Make regular backups

Backup your wallet on a regular basis so that every recent Bitcoin change of addresses and all new Bitcoin addresses you created are included in your backup. However, all applications will be soon using wallets that only need to be backed up once.

Encrypt your wallet

Encrypting your wallet with a password protects you against thieves or against anyone trying to withdraw any funds. This helps protect against thieves, though it cannot protect against key logging hardware or software.

Never forget your password

It is very important to remember your password, or your funds will permanently lost. Since Bitcoin is so secure, there are very minimal password recovery options with Bitcoin. It is important to make a password that you will be able to remember many years later even if you haven't used it. For more certainty, keep a paper copy of your password in a safe place like a vault.

Use a strong password

Make your password at least 16 characters long with a combination of letters, numbers, punctuation marks to make it strong. You can generate very secure passwords by programs designed specifically for strong password creation. Strong passwords are harder to remember, so take care in memorizing it or write it down.

Offline wallet for savings

Offline wallets are often referred to as cold storages. These types are highly secured and best for savings. It securely stores your wallet offline. This type offers the best protection against computer vulnerabilities if stored properly. Using an offline wallet in combination with backups and encryption is also a good idea. Here is an overview of some approaches.

Offline transaction signing

Hardware wallets

Keep your software up to date

Keeping your Bitcoin software up to date enables you to receive important stability and security fixes. Timely Updates can instantly prevent mega problems, install new useful features and help keep your wallet safe. Installing updates for all other software on your computer or mobile is also important to keep your wallet environment safer.

Multi-signature to protect against theft

Bitcoin includes a multi-signature feature that allows a transaction to require multiple independent approvals to be spent. This comes in handy for big organizations that give its members access to its assets while only allowing a withdrawal of 3 of 5 members sign the transaction. Some web wallets also provide multi-signature wallets, giving the user all control over their money while preventing a thief from stealing funds by compromising a single device or server.

Think about your testament

Without a backup plan for peers and family, you can easily lose all your bitcoins forever. Never trust everyone with your passwords, but make sure you take some time to pen down what you want to be done with your bitcoins and who should get your passwords and keys. Not taking care of these things can result in a loss of your bitcoins forever.

CHAPTER 9: Trading

Crypto currencies are growing vast. In 2017 bitcoin (BTC) grew from $1,000/BTC to over $16,000/BTC. This growth results in an explosion in market trading, which in turn keeps the growth curve increasing.

This is great for starting investors because they don't need their own crypto currency wallet, and can get a feel for the market movements without needing to buy it outright.

How to trade cryptocurrencies without trading experience?

Copy Trading – *" The facebook of trading"*

Copy trading provides the opportunity to automatically copy positions opened and managed by an investor of their choice, usually in the context of a social trading network. The copying trader usually retains the ability to disconnect copied trades and manage themselves. One of the most famous platform available currently is eToro

However, lately we notice an increase in copy trading platforms created specifically for the crytocurrency trading enthusiast. The fund raised to support its operation is obviously through ICO.

How to pick a trading platform

Trading platforms are not all the same, here are some main differences:

The currencies available: Bitcoin to USD is widely available, but other fiat and cryptocurrencies might not be available on all platforms.

Leverage available: Leverage lets you trade beyond your initial deposit and multiply your gains. This is best suited for those who prefer higher risks and rewards. You can often find leverage up to 20:1 with cryptocurrency, depending on your chosen platform and currency pair.

Trading features: Hedging, stop-loss features and other options can give you more control over your trading. Experienced traders might be able to benefit from these, while first-timers might prefer to keep it simple.

Minimum investment: What's the minimum (and maximum) amount you can invest? Does it work for you?

A word on risk

Market trading of any asset is risky, and while cryptocurrencies are highly profitable they are also very volatile, thus a return on investment is never a guarantee. There is no guarantee of a return of investment. It is wise not to trade with capital you can't afford to lose.

How cryptocurrency trading works

Market trading in 2017 is accessible for everyone not just for the elite. Cryptocurrency will keep growing since it goes hand in hand with the growth of online currency exchanges and trading platforms where anyone can take part and profit from market speculation. You just need to know how it works.

What is forex market trading?

Foreign exchange (forex) market trading is the act of purchasing and selling currencies between traders. In its simplest form, you're betting on the changing price difference between two different currencies.

To partake in forex trading you need to open an account and deposit funds into it. These funds are then used to place buy and sell orders against another currency. The only way to make profits is to sell or close orders at a higher price than you bought.

How do you make a profit?

To start trading you deposit funds into your account. When you bet correctly the funds in your account increase. When you bet incorrectly, the funds in your account decrease.

With leverage, you can magnify your profits and losses.

For example, say you placed a US$1,000 trade on bitcoin increasing in price, without leverage. If its price increased by 10%, compared to the US dollar, during the trade period your profits would be $100, minus any trading fees.But if you traded with 10:1 leverage, your profits would be 10 times that, minus the trading fees.As you can see, the sharp price movements of cryptocurrencies, combined with leverage, can quickly produce substantial returns. However, it goes both ways. If the price starts dropping, leverage might chew through your deposited funds quickly.

Cryptocurrency trading

Trading cryptocurrencies work exactly the same, but instead of selling and buying fiat currencies, such as euros or US dollars, traders buy and sell cryptocurrencies, such as bitcoin, Ethereum or Litecoin. For example, you might bet on the changing price difference between the US dollar and bitcoin. Or you might bet on the changing values between two different cryptocurrencies, such as by trading a BTC:ETH pair. If you think bitcoin will increase in value, you might "go long" on it. This means betting that it will increase in value relative to the US dollar. If you think bitcoin will decrease in value, you might "short" it instead. This means betting that it will decrease in value relative to the US dollar.You're not actually buying the cryptocurrency. Instead, you're just placing an order on the market. Just like forex market trading, cryptocurrency trading works by exchanging one currency into another and back. You will usually exchange a fiat currency into a cryptocurrency and then, at a later date, back into a fiat currency, although there are traders and exchanges that allow cryptocurrency-to-cryptocurrency trading.

For example, let's take a look at the BTC to USD chart for 2017:

Bitcoin to USD price chart, January 2017 – December 2017 (Yahoo Finance)

We can see here, that as 2017 progressed, the value of bitcoin exploded in comparison with the dollar, growing from just under $1,000/BTC on 1 January 2017 to over $10,800/BTC in the last week of November 2017.

Types of traders

There are two types of trading available to traders interested in market trading cryptocurrencies:

Short-term trading (day trading)

Short-term trading eschews the stability of long-term trading for the possibility of taking advantage of short-term price swings and involves buying and selling cryptocurrencies over the span of a day or a few hours. If you'd rather take advantage of the characteristic volatility of cryptocurrencies by getting in and out of a trade quickly, then this method might be for you. Technical analysis becomes handy to you as you must be able to time the best entry or exit points based on the chart pattern.

Long-term trading (investing)

Long-term traders buy and hold cryptocurrencies over a long period. They may hold a cryptocurrency for weeks, months or even years. Studying price trends over a long period allows long-term traders to make informed decisions and avoid suffering from short-term dips in value. If you believe the value of a cryptocurrency will grow steadily over a long period and don't want the stress that comes from short-term value dips, then this method might be your best choice.

The advantages of trading cryptocurrencies

Trading cryptocurrencies, while similar to trading fiat currencies on forex, comes with its own set of advantages.

Cheaper fees and fast exchanges: For each trade, the exchange platform you're using will take a small percentage as commission for the service they're providing. This is inevitable. Where cryptocurrency trades differ from their fiat currency equivalent is in the size of this fee. Because the fees for transferring cryptocurrencies (typically via wallet payments) are cheaper than credit card and bank transfer fees, market-trading fees are cheaper than forex-trading fees.

Open all week: You can only trade stocks and commodities during business hours, and you can often only trade forex during weekdays. Cryptocurrencies, on the other hand, can be traded 24/7, anytime and anywhere, depending on the exchange.

Extreme volatility: Traders make profits when the price of the currency takes large strides upwards, and cryptocurrencies often experience large price movements. While this increases the risk (large price movements happen downwards as well), you can often make a lot of profit with a relatively small bankroll.

Risk and things to watch

If you're not careful when it comes to cryptocurrency trading, you could find yourself gambling more than you're trading, and eventually, you might lose everything you've invested. Trading is not a game, and just as there is real money to be made, there is real money to be lost. Doing your research and keeping the following concepts in mind when trading could help you avoid the pitfalls of cryptocurrency trading.

Cryptocurrency's volatility

The number one thing you'll need to keep in mind when it comes to cryptocurrency trading is that the price is extremely volatile. Where certain trade techniques used in forex might take months to come to see gains, in cryptocurrency trading, it could only take hours or days. While this is beneficial when it comes to making a profit, it could also be your downfall if the price moves the other way.

Patterns sometimes lie

Many market-trading books and guides cover certain chart-reading techniques and patterns used to predict the market by professionals. While the market does sometimes follow patterns, this is never a guaranteed outcome, and unless you limit your exposure, you could end up losing a lot of money over a pattern that does not exist.

Limit your exposure

Limiting your exposure comes down to two specific concepts:

Never invest more money than you are willing to lose
You should consider any money you put into a trade as lost. If you're uncomfortable with this notion, then you're trading more money than you should be. Finding the point where you're comfortable with this concept is key to helping you trade stress-free.

Consider setting up "take profit" and "stop loss" orders
These limits are offered by many professional trading platforms and can automatically liquidate and "cash out" your position at predefined prices.

Stay away from leverage

Leverage is money that a broker loans you. It's wise to stay away from leverage until you've learned everything you can learn about making trades with your own money. While leverage can help you make greater profits with short cryptocurrency movements, it can also amplify your losses when the trade takes a wrong turn.

Leverage example

You decide to trade $1000 dollars to BTC. Additionally, you leverage another $10,000 from your broker. Now you can buy 1.0 BTC at $11,000/BTC. Later you sell at $13,000/BTC, return the $10,000 and you are left with $3,000, a profit of $2,000 on your initial $1,000. Unfortunately, this works the other way around. If the price of bitcoin had fallen to $5,000/BTC instead, you would have lost $6,000. Always remember, leverage amplifies your winnings and your losses equally. As a beginner, the risks presented when using leverage are just not worth the possibility of amplified profits.

Know when to exit and cash out

What market trading really comes down to is knowing when to close a trade. This is the crux of the operation. Getting into a trade is easy, knowing when to get out is hard, and that is where you should focus most of your learning. This again involves two different aspects:

Closing a trade in profit: It is important to take your winnings out of a trade. Cryptocurrencies can move down more quickly than they move up and you don't want to be late cashing out of a trade. You also don't want to be too early and miss out on extra profits. There are a lot of techniques to help you make this decision that are out of the scope of this beginner's guide.

Cutting your losses: Similarly, you want to be ready to cut your losses if a trade goes too wrong while also not getting out too early in case the cryptocurrency recovers. Again, there are countless guides and books to help you make this decision.

How to get started trading cryptocurrency

Some trading platforms will suit your needs much better than others. It's worth comparing them in detail and trying demos where available to find the one you like.

	Details	Features
BITFINEX Bitfinex Multi-coin Exchange	Spot trade all of the major cryptos on this full-featured exchange and margin trading platform. View a demo before you get started.	• **Fees:** Range from 0%-0.2% • **Supported countries:** Worldwide

Details		Features
		Payment methods: Cryptocurrencies, USD, EUR
BINANCE Binance Cryptocurrency Exchange	Trade 60+ cryptocurrency pairs on this up-and-coming exchange based in China. Multi-language support.	• **Trade Bitcoin Cash & Bitcoin Gold** • **Fees:** 0.1% trading fee • **Supported countries:** Worldwide **Deposit methods:** BTC, ETH, LTC, NEO & BNB
eToro eToro Social Crypto Trading	Copy the trades of leading cryptocurrency investors on this unique social investment platform.	• **Fees:** Spreads • **Supported countries:** Worldwide (some exceptions) • **Payment methods:** Credit card, PayPal, bank transfer

Source: www.finder.com

This information should not be interpreted as an endorsement of cryptocurrencies or a recommendation to invest. Historic performance is no guarantee of future returns. As an investment class, cryptocurrencies are speculative investments and investing in cryptocurrencies involves significant risks – they are highly volatile, vulnerable to hacking and capital loss and sensitive to secondary activity. Before investing you should obtain advice and decide whether the potential return outweighs the risks. This information should not be interpreted as an endorsement of cryptocurrencies or a recommendation to invest. Historic performance is no guarantee of future returns. As an investment class, cryptocurrencies are speculative investments and investing in cryptocurrencies involves significant risks – they are highly volatile, vulnerable to hacking and capital loss and sensitive to secondary activity. Before investing you should obtain advice and decide whether the potential return outweighs the risks. This information should not be interpreted as an endorsement of cryptocurrencies or a recommendation to invest. Historic performance is no guarantee of future returns. As an investment class, cryptocurrencies are speculative investments and investing in cryptocurrencies involves significant risks – they are highly volatile, vulnerable to hacking and capital loss and sensitive to secondary activity. Before investing you should obtain advice and decide whether the potential return outweighs the risks.

This information should not be interpreted as an endorsement of cryptocurrencies or a recommendation to invest. Historic performance is no guarantee of future returns. As an investment class, cryptocurrencies are speculative investments and investing in cryptocurrencies involves significant risks – they are highly volatile, vulnerable to hacking and capital loss and sensitive to secondary activity. Before investing you should obtain advice and decide whether the potential return outweighs the riskThis information should not be interpreted as an endorsement of cryptocurrencies or a recommendation to invest. Historic performance is no guarantee of future returns. As an investment class, cryptocurrencies are speculative investments and investing in cryptocurrencies involves significant risks – they are highly volatile, vulnerable to hacking and capital loss and sensitive to secondary activity. Before investing you should obtain advice and decide whether the potential return outweighs the risks.This information should not be interpreted as an endorsement of cryptocurrencies or a recommendation to invest. Historic performance is no guarantee of future returns. As an investment class, cryptocurrencies are speculative investments and investing in cryptocurrencies involves significant risks – they are highly volatile, vulnerable to hacking and capital loss and sensitive to secondary activity. Before investing you should obtain advice and decide whether the potential return outweighs the risks.This information should not be interpreted as an endorsement of cryptocurrencies or a recommendation to invest. Historic performance is no guarantee of future returns. As an investment class, cryptocurrencies are speculative investments and investing in cryptocurrencies involves significant risks – they are highly volatile, vulnerable to hacking and capital loss and sensitive to secondary activity. Before investing you should obtain advice and decide whether the potential return outweighs the risks.Bottom of Form

After that:

Step 1. Learn the platform

Cryptocurrency brokers usually offer their own trading platform, and each broker's system will be slightly different from one another. You will need to put in the time to learn how the platform works, where each feature is and how to utilize it. When you first access a broker's trading platform, you might feel overwhelmed. This is normal. Spend some time with it and continue doing your research. You will get comfortable with it in no time.

Step 2. Timing?

The old adage of "buy low, sell high" holds for cryptocurrencies just as it holds for any other sort of investment or trading. Cryptocurrency markets move up and down, and large movements up are often followed by sudden dips. Learning of some basic technical analysis skills to study candlestick charts like below is useful to time your entry and also to gauge your take profit or stop loss.

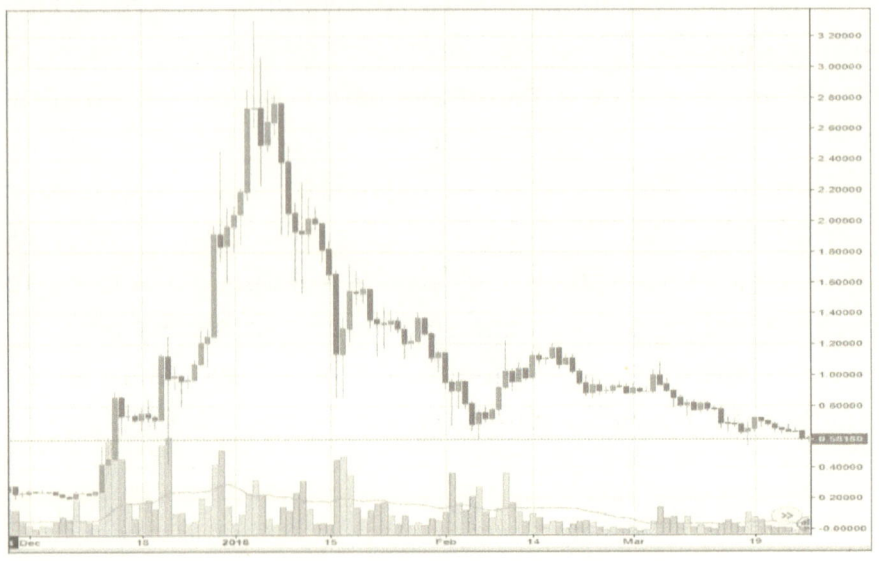

Ripple to USD/XRPUSD price chart, Dec 2017 – March 2018 (Tradingview)

Step 4. Training makes perfect

The best way to learn how to trade is to actually trade. There is no secret. Once you've learned all the theory, you'll need to get your feet wet. Buy some cryptocurrency, set your limits and get started. Just remember that it's almost similar to gambling. Go in expecting to lose your money, and you'll never be disappointed.

What affects the price of a cryptocurrency?

Cryptocurrencies are volatile by nature. They are not as stable as currencies that have had centuries to develop. Bitcoin is the oldest coin on the market, and it has only been around since 2009. Nevertheless, there are a number of things that can affect cryptocurrencies:

Regulation: If a government makes a statement or pushes for a particular regulation that affects cryptocurrencies, you can bet that the price will react to it (sometimes positively, often negatively). When China banned ICOs, the price of Ethereum fell by 41% in 15 days (from$386.83/ETH to $228.06).

Media influence: Just like government regulation, exposure in the media greatly affects a cryptocurrency's price. Whenever a public figure makes a statement regarding cryptocurrencies, or a major retailer starts accepting cryptocurrency as a form of payment, you will see the market respond.

Changes to the technology: When a cryptocurrency's core technology is affected (either via an update or the finding of a flaw), the cryptocurrency's price is also affected.

Trading cryptocurrencies works almost exactly the same as trading fiat currencies, and it will benefit you greatly to learn the theory behind trading currencies. While profits are never guaranteed when trading, you can take steps to protect yourself from heavy losses and to improve your understanding of how markets move.

There's more to know than can be crammed into this guide, but the only real way to learn is by doing. This generally means picking a platform, setting aside some money that you don't mind losing, and getting started to trade cryptoassets!

CHAPTER10: Regulatory and Tax Treatment

USA

In 2013 the U.S. treasury acknowledged bitcoin a convertible decentralized virtual currency. In September 2015, the Commodity Futures Trading Commission, CFTC, named bitcoin a commodity. The IRS taxes bitcoin as a property, yet in 2016 a federal judge ruled that "Bitcoins are funds within the plain meaning of that term. Since then it is expected that there will be similar regulations in Canada and Mexico. jurisdiction: https://en.wikipedia.org/wiki/Legality_of_Bitcoin_by_U.S._jurisdiction BitLicense: A business license issued by the New York State Department of Financial Services applicable to those conducting business in the state of New York. The application cost is approximately $100,000 Required, if business activity involves: Receiving virtual currency (VC) for Transmission or Transmitting VC, unless for non-financial purposes and only a nominal amount of VC; Storing, holding, or maintaining custody or control of VC on behalf of others; Buying and selling VC a customer business; Performing Exchange Services as a customer business; Controlling, administering, or issuing a VC

In September 2017, Circle, Ripple and Coinbase also received the BitLicense.

Taxation: USA

According to IRS – all "virtual currencies", used for tax purposes fall under the section "property". Virtual currency is prone to long-term and short-term capital gains / losses upon realization / sale.

Income and expenses in digital currencies are taxed and reportable as per regular standards.

Currency earned through mining is treated as ordinary income.

This guidance fell in favor of investors of digital currency eventhough there were some difficulties for consumers using digital currency in the beginning stages.

Sales tax did not fall under the IRS, since the IRS id the federal tax agency and sales tax is regulated by the individual states. IRS' recent collaboration with Chainanalysis to identify tax evaders: https://www.cryptocoinsnews.com/irs-tracked-bitcoin-tax-evaders-since-2015/

When making this decision, the IRS decided that every time you purchase something with, say, a bitcoin you have "sold" bitcoin and therefore have to calculate a capital gain or loss relative to your "basis" (purchase price) of the bitcoins you sold.   There is no minimum exemption.

This Law would not work with traditional currency because the record-keeping requirements would be overwhelming. Since bitcoin's transaction only happens online, a software can easily calculate all these gains or losses automatically, nevertheless, this still might form a hindrance to consumers in the future.

Opting for a more traditional treatment of Bitcoin would still not, in and of itself, eliminate these issues. It should be mandatory that corporations report foreign currency gains / losses as do individuals

Taxation: USA and what is different in EU

Consider this a prime example of how the complex nature of crypto currency digital currency does not mix well with existing laws. One can only hope that there is political push to make some exemptions for digital currency and to encourage its usage just like it was previously done with e-commerce (e-commerce was exempted from local and state sales tax given the perceived practical difficulties at the time of correctly calculating these taxes in the early days of the internet)

On the other side, one must admit that the prospect of citizens making online transactions on an ongoing basis in a digital currency (say Bitcoin) presents its own set of taxation challenges that are different than the normal de minimus use of foreign currency on vacation

In EU on the other hand, in October 22, 2015, a court ruling for ECJ judged that bitcoin transactions "are exempt from VAT under the provision concerning transactions relating to currency, bank notes and coins used as legal tender." This change was met with enthusiasm from European exchanges that dwelled in uncertainty on their VAT obligations thus far, and openly enables increased adoption as a payment method.

The European Union

In 2014 the European Central Bank acknowledges bitcoin as a convertible decentralized virtual currency. In July of that same year, the European Banking Authority warned European banks not to deal in virtual currencies such as bitcoin until a regulatory regime was set. In 2015 the European Union collectively didn't pass any specific legislation relating to the status of the bitcoin as a currency, but has stated in October 2015 that VAT/GST has no direct impact on the conversion between traditional fiat currency and bitcoin. VAT/GST and other taxes such as income tax still apply to transactions made using bitcoins for goods and services. In 2016: The European Parliament's passed a proposal requesting a taskforce to scan virtual currencies in an attempt to fight money laundering and terrorism. This proposal has been sent to the European Commission for consideration. In 2017 a proposal emtailing cryptocurrency exchanges and cryptocurrency wallets to record suspicious actions was presented by the European commission

Europe

Not regulated but legal:

Cyprus, Croatia, Czech Republic, Poland, Romania, Slovakia, Denmark, Estonia Russia, Bulgaria, Greece, Italy, Malta, Portugal, Turkey, Belgium, Ireland, Netherlands

Regulated and legal:

Germany: "Unit of account" and can be used for tax and trading

UK: cryptocurrency is treated as private money, no VAT for exchanging BTC to fiat. The VAT is pertinent for goods and services sold for BTC or any other cryptocurrency. Relevant profits/losses subject to capital gains tax

Slovenia: Here mining and businesses selling goods and services in bitcoin are taxed.

Switzerland: Businesses handling Bitcoins are subject to anti-money laundering regulations and may need a banking license

Norway: this country views Bitcoin as an asset thus falls under the sales tax regulation

Sweden: Subject to Financial Supervisory Authority regulations and treated as currency

France: Regulations issued for exchanges, taxation and businesses

South America

Legal Argentina, Brazil, Chile, Colombia

Illegal:

Bolivia: In 2014 bitcoin was abruptly banned by The Central Bank of Bolivia. Moreover, 60 cryptocurrency promoters were arrested in May 2017.

Ecuador: The government banned bitcoin and other cryptocurrency activities in 2014, however use of Bitcoin still grows until now.

Asia

Legal:

The governments in Saudi Arabia, Lebanon and Jordan have issued warnings on the use of Bitcoins; nevertheless it is still legal. India has no plans to regulate cryptocurrencies. China allows individuals to hold and trade cryptocurrencies but prohibits financial institutions from doing the same. Japan recognizes cryptocurrencies as a method of payment

Illegal and/or non regulated:

Kyrgyzstan, Bangladesh: Illegal

China: Prohibition on Bitcoin activities by any financial institutions caused Bitcoin trading to sink. On 11 January 2017 the central bank announced investigations into Bitcoin exchanges in Beijing and Shanghai. Looking at unlawful activities, such as money laundering, margin trading, and transferring funds abroad. Prices fell 10%. On January 22, China's three largest exchanges ended free Bitcoin trading to curb speculation. Bitcoin trading dropped further due to fees imposed. On February 9, the PBoC met with nine Bitcoin exchanges to remind them of potential risks. The two largest exchanges, OkCoin and Huobi.com, temporarily halted withdrawals from their platforms. BTCChina also announced a 72hour waiting period for withdrawals. China's recent ICO ban affected many startups which now look oversees to list their tokens

Malaysia: Bitcoin is not recognised as legal tender in Malaysia.The Central Bank does not regulate the operations of Bitcoin. However, the country is planning to introduce its own regulatory framework for cryptocurrencies. The Central Bank of Malaysia is looking into designating all cryptocurrency exchanges as "reporting institutions" under Amla beginning 2018

Taxation

United Kingdom: Treat as any other foreign currency Not VAT-able, a reversal of its prior decision that it was a VAT-able voucher In early November 2014, a Call for Information was issued to gauge the opinions of participants in the economy on regulation and taxation In a more recent announcement, the FCA announced the creation of a regulatory sandbox for Bitcoin and Ethereum companies in an attempt to bring them close to digital currency businesses.

In March 2015, the UK Treasury published its plans to regulate Bitcoin, also noting the potential advantages of digital currencies as a payments technology. Among their plans are to: Apply Anti-Money Laundering (AML) regulation to digital currency exchanges in the UK for the purpose of supporting innovation and for prevention of criminal use. Work with the British Standards Institution (BSI) and the digital currency industry to develop standards for consumer protection. Increase digital currency research funding by £10M and bring together various research councils, the Alan Turing Institute and Digital Catapult with industry, in order to research digital currency technology opportunities and challenges

France: The French Ministry of Economy and Finance announced in July 2014 that measures and taxes were to be placed until the end of the year, although not recognizing digital currencies as official currencies. A threshold is to be placed at €5,000, so that people can "try, invest and develop business with Bitcoin", before it becomes subject to taxes. Robert Ophele, president of the Autorite des marches financiers (AMF), the domestic financial markets regulator, said that soon his agency is planning to finalize regulations on ICOs Japan JADA (Japan Authority of Digital Asset) was formulated to create and establish standards, best practices and guidelines and offer advice and consultancy, for the safe and sound operation of its members. In 2014, the Japanese government made a decision that did not recognize bitcoin as currency nor bond under the current Banking Act and Financial Instruments and Exchange Law, prohibiting banks and securities companies from dealing in bitcoins. In 2017, the country's government officially recognized bitcoin as a method of payment.

Brazil: Treat as a financial asset subject to 15% capital gains tax (reference) As such, bitcoins must be filed as an income tax return on how much they are worth and how much profit was made Receita Federal (the Federal Revenue service) decided that bitcoins must be declared as "other goods" when their value is higher than BRL 1,000 When more than BRL 35,000 worth in bitcoins is earned as profit, it is subject to income tax Central bank's president Ilan Goldfajn, recently compared Bitcoin to a pyramid scheme, even though legislators in Brazil seem to work out a regulatory framework for domestic cryptocurrency activities. Australia In August 2014, ATO defined that Bitcoin and all digital currencies are subject to existing Goods and Services Tax (GST) for sales and Capital Gains Tax (CGT), similarly to equities and other assets (for sums over $10,000); In April 2015, the Reserve Bank of Australia (RBA) indicated that it is not in favor of regulating Bitcoin or other digital currencies, since "any benefits of regulation would outweigh the costs". They also stated that, "...digital currencies don't raise concerns with regards to competition, efficiency or risk to the financial system". However, now it seems that regulations are close to being imposed. The use, trading and mining of Bitcoins is legal and the Australian Taxation office has announced its intention to establish guidelines on VAT and capital gains tax

Denmark :Denmark's Financial Supervisory Authority (Finanstilsynet) rejects bitcoin as a currency and stated that it will not regulate bitcoins Personal gains and losses from trading digital currency are not taxable (or tax-deductible) Corporations whose primary business is digital currency trading are taxable The FSA has now suggested amending the present legislation so that virtual currencies and regulation come under their remit.

Finland: The Finish Tax Authority has issued instructions for the taxation of Bitcoin and other digital currencies When transferred to another currency, the rules on taxation of capital gains apply When the currency is used as a form of payment for goods and services, it is treated as a trade, and the increase in value that the currency might have gained after it was obtained is taxable Losses are not-tax deductible A bitcoin transaction is considered a private contract equivalent to a contract for difference for tax purposes

Russia: Issued warnings in January 2014 that the use of currencies besides the ruble is illegal, and has since proceeded to release draft bills with the penalties involved for the promotion and use of "money surrogates" like Bitcoin. The Russian Central Bank views the services of Russian legal entities aimed at assisting in the exchange of bitcoins for goods, services, or currencies as a "dubious activity" associated with money laundering and terrorism financing One update from Russian Central Bank's governor : "…this is something definitely the market will be welcoming so we will be watching with attention and, if necessary, regulate it." Following a meeting with Vladimir Putin, Russian regulators announced that cryptocurrencies will officially be regulated in Russia. A framework is expected to be established by the end of 2017 as a joint effort of the central bank and the finance ministry.

Useful Website

Bitcoin white paper by Satoshi Nakamoto

Ethereum white paper by Vitalik Buterin

Coin Market Cap (information about price performance and market capitalization of cryptocurrencies / tokens)

Coin Spectator (this site aggregates cryptocurrency-related news from over 100 sources and it is my one stop shop site to make sure I don't miss anything important)

Etherscan.io - check Ether transactions

Blockchain.info – check Bitcoin transactions

Blockgeeks - a leading online learning platform that helps anyone learn Blockchain in business, software, technology and creative skills

FAQ

Will blockchain collapsed?
not likely, only if something drastic happens like launching nuclear destroying the entire globe, but then all of us would be dead or dying anyway. Even under such drastic circumstances you technically still would have your bitcoins if you stored it in a paper wallet. You'll just have to find an electronic device that can read it.

Do you always have to buy a whole coin?
Not at all, you can also buy just a fraction of a coin fraction such as 0.1 0.0250, 0.01365 subject to the minimum transaction amount of your wallet or exchange.

Which is the best cryptocurrency to invest in today?
To each it's own, but I believe that the best cryptocurrency to purchase is one we believe in even if it goes down.

How to determine a good ICO?
Solid team with the member's profile publish on Linked, an idea that has real, plausible implementation for blockchain use, good prelaunch social media channels available as well as good customer service. Avoid ICOs that promised high return and confusing white paper content.

What is the main difference between tokens and cryptocurrencies?
Currency is always an accepted form of money. It can be paper notes or coins, these are issued by the government and then circulated in the economy. Cryptocurrency on the other hand is not that different from tokens. Tokens are issued by enthusiastic developers to the community to be

either bought or received for something in return. You can also trade token, then it becomes a cryptocurrency.